Quick Start Guides

C000095221

The Essential
15 MINUTE
MEALS
Cookbook For Weight Loss

Fast and Easy

Calorie-Counted

Recipes

Lose Weight Quickly With Delicious Healthy Meals

First published in 2021 by Erin Rose Publishing

Text and illustration copyright © 2021 Erin Rose Publishing

Design: Julie Anson

DISCLAIMER: This book is for informational purposes only and not intended as a substitute for the medical advice, diagnosis or treatment of a physician or qualified healthcare provider. The reader should consult a physician before undertaking a new health care regime and in all matters relating to his/her health, and particularly with respect to any symptoms that may require diagnosis or medical attention.

While every care has been taken in compiling the recipes for this book we cannot accept responsibility for any problems which arise as a result of preparing one of the recipes. The author and publisher disclaim responsibility for any adverse effects that may arise from the use or application of the recipes in this book. Some of the recipes in this book include nuts and eggs. If you have an egg or nut allergy it's important to avoid these. It is recommended that children, pregnant women, the elderly or anyone who has an immune system disorder avoid eating raw eggs.

CONTENTS

Introduction...1

Top Tips For Fast Easy Cooking 2

Breakfast Recipes..3

Coffee & Nut Butter Protein Shake 4

Chocolate Protein Shake 5

Summer Berry Smoothie...6

Strawberry & Avocado Smoothie 7

Apple & Ginger Smoothie...8

Detox Smoothie 9

Apple & Lime Shots..10

Kiwi Salad Shots 11

Pear Salad Smoothie..12

Superfood Juice 13

Green Goodness Smoothie 14

Avocado & Banana Smoothie 15

Raspberry & Cashew Nut Crunch...........................16

Ham & Tomato Mug Muffin.....................................17

Mushroom & Herb Omelette 18

Raspberry & Lemon Swirl 19

Poached Eggs & Spinach 20

Herby Mediterranean Scramble..............................21

Coconut & Lemon Yogurt 22

Chocolate & Macadamia Yogurt 23

Lunch Recipes...25

Prawn & Basil Savoury Muffin 26

Cheese & Olive Frittata 27

Chorizo Scramble..28

Paprika Prawn Tapas 29

Parmesan Asparagus..30

Asparagus & Poached Egg 31

Mediterranean Tomato & Lentil Soup.......................................32

Red Pepper & Basil Soup 33

Beef & Mushroom Soup 34

Fast Tomato Soup 35

Green Vegetable Soup...36

Red Pepper & Chickpea Soup 37

Gazpacho 38

Egg Drop Soup 39

Asparagus Soup..40

Creamy Chicken & Vegetable Soup 41

Avocado, Lime & Coriander (Cilantro) Soup 42

Turkey Soup 43

Red Pepper & Cannellini Soup 44

Cannellini & Courgette Soup 45

Creamy Tomato & Pesto Soup 46

Quick Chicken & Mushroom Soup 47

Cucumber, Lettuce & Pea Soup..48

Chilli Tomato King Prawns..49

Serrano & Rocket Salad...50

Lemon & Pine Nut Asparagus..51

Smokey Bean & Quinoa Salad 52

Beetroot & Lentil Salad 53

Sweetcorn & Bean Salad 54

Grapefruit & Pine Nut Salad..55

Feta & Watermelon Salad 56

Tuna & Cannellini Bean Salad...57

Greek Chicken Salad 58

Chilli Turkey & Avocado Salad...59

Chickpea, Lemon & Coriander Salad..................................60

Feta Cheese & Butterbean Salad 61

Quick Bean Chilli 62

Spanish Rice 63

Dinner Recipes 65

Chicken Fajitas, Salsa & Lettuce Wrap...............................66

Surf & Turf Steak With Prawns And Garlic Sauce................67

Chicken With Vegetable 'Spaghetti' 68

Tuna Steaks With Olives, Lemon & Basil Dressing 69

Scallops & Pancetta 70

Pork Béarnaise...71

Lemon Mustard Salmon & Lentils 72

Pomegranate, Avocado & Chicken Salad 73

Turkey Satay Skewers 74

Hazelnut Crusted Salmon 75

Creamy Parmesan Chicken 76

Prawn, Avocado & Cannellini Salad 77

Tomato & Herb Chicken 78

Creamy Turkey & Leeks...79

Creamy Avocado 'Courgetti'..80

Smokey Bean Casserole 81

Prawn & Chorizo Stir-Fry 82

Chicken & Green Peppers..83

Garlic Prawns & Calamari..84

Lemon & Basil Chicken Skewers 85

Smoked Salmon & Chicory Scoops 86

Tomato & Mozzarella Skewers 87

Barbecued Mushrooms 88

Mushroom Stroganoff 89

Desserts, Treats & Snacks Recipes 91

Blueberry, Coconut & Chia Seed Pudding 92

Passion Fruit & Raspberry Mascarpone 93

Iced Banana & Choc Chip Cream 94

Apple & Caramel Dip 95

Rhubarb & Ginger Compote With Greek Yogurt 96

Banana Frappuccino 97

Coconut Balls 98

Cherry & Chocolate Milkshake 99

Introduction

If you are looking for healthy weight loss recipes that are delicious, easy and ready in 15 minutes then look no further!

This **Quick Start Guide** provides you with plenty of calorie counted, low carb recipes which are ideal for weight loss. You can enjoy great tasting food which keeps you feeling fuller for longer.

Even if you don't have much time you can have slimming foods which are suitable for many different diets, including sugar-free, low carb, calorie counting and intermittent fasting which helps you optimise your health and weight loss.

This quick and easy cookbook contains recipes which are simple to follow. The recipes are listed under breakfast, lunch, dinner and desserts but you can interchange them to suit your lifestyle and dietary needs. With so many fast and tasty recipes to choose from you can expand your range of slimming meals and not spend too much time in the kitchen.

Cooking with fresh ingredients allows you to avoid hidden sugars, unhealthy fats and additives which hamper weight loss. So if you have difficulty losing weight your body could benefit from a healthier, home cooked diet.

Are you ready to kick start your weight loss and improve your health? Let's get started!

> **Always check with your doctor before making significant changes to your diet to check it's safe for you to do so, especially if you have any health issues or underlying conditions.**

Top Tips For Fast Easy Cooking

Make good use of leftover food and you can create a quick and tasty omelette, stir-fry or soup without any fuss. Eggs add so much variety with omelettes and scrambles and they add protein if you don't have meat available.

Chopping vegetables and meats into smaller pieces will reduce the cooking time. Improvise with your ingredients. If you don't have a particular ingredient in the cupboard, make a substitution for something similar, like kale instead of spinach.

Keep an abundant supply of key ingredients as store cupboard essentials, such as tinned and frozen goods. Ready cooked pulses and beans, tinned tomatoes, tuna, stock (broth) and vegetables are a great resource and backup if your fridge is getting low. Yes, fresh is best but frozen vegetables are a great substitute without losing too many of the nutrients.

Batch cooking larger portions of a meal which can be stored in the freezer means you can save time later with a quick healthy meal which can be defrosted. Remember to label your freezer bags or containers so you can easily identify the contents.

Pre-prepared vegetables which have been washed, peeled and chopped ready for cooking are handy to have in the fridge although some find the taste is not quite the same.

Ready cooked chicken and meat bought from the supermarket means you can literally assemble a meal using salad leaves or add it to soups and stir-fries to save time. Mason jars are not only a great way of storing and transporting foods such as carrying salads to work, they can also be put in the microwave for warm-up lunches.

BREAKFAST RECIPES

Coffee & Nut Butter Protein Shake

SERVES 1

224 calories per serving

Ingredients

1 teaspoon instant coffee powder

1 teaspoon smooth peanut butter

1 tablespoon vanilla protein powder (sugar-free)

250mls (8fl oz) milk (or milk alternative)

Several ice cubes

Method

Place all of the ingredients into blender or food processor and blitz until smooth. Serve into a glass and enjoy!

Chocolate Protein Shake

Ingredients

1 teaspoon 100% cocoa powder

1 teaspoon peanut butter

2 teaspoons vanilla protein powder (sugar-free)

200mls (7fl oz) almond milk (or other milk alternative)

Several ice cubes

SERVES 1

115 calories per serving

Method

Place all of the ingredients into blender or food processor and blitz until smooth. Serve into a glass and enjoy!

Summer Berry Smoothie

Ingredients

100g (3½ oz) mixed summer berries;
blueberries, raspberries, redcurrants,
blackberries etc.

1 carrot

1 small orange

SERVES 1

107
calories
per serving

Method

Place all the ingredients into a blender with enough water to cover them and process until smooth.

Strawberry & Avocado Smoothie

SERVES 1

187 calories per serving

Ingredients

100g (3½oz) strawberries, hulled

½ avocado, stone removed and peeled

100mls (3½fl oz) coconut water

Squeeze of lemon juice

Method

Toss all of the ingredients into a food processor and blitz until smooth and creamy. You can add a little water if you like it less thick.

Apple & Ginger Smoothie

Ingredients

1 carrot, peeled and chopped

1 apple, cored and chopped

2.5cm (1 inch) piece of ginger root, peeled

SERVES 1

84 calories per serving

Method

Place all of the ingredients into a blender with enough water to cover them. Blitz until smooth. Serve and drink straight away.

Detox Smoothie

53
calories
per serving

Ingredients

½ bulb of fennel, chopped

½ cucumber, chopped

1 stalk of celery

Juice of 1 lemon

Method

Place the fennel, cucumber and celery into a food processor or smoothie maker and add the lemon juice together with enough water to cover the ingredients. Process until smooth.

Apple & Lime Shots

Ingredients

3 kale leaves

5 sprigs of mint

Juice of 2 limes

2 apples

1 cucumber

SERVES 1

152 calories per serving

Method

Place the lime juice, apples, cucumber, kale and mint into a juicer and extract the juice. Alternatively, use a blender and add sufficient water to cover the ingredients. Store in a bottle in the fridge. You can take healthy shots throughout the day or you can just drink it all straight away.

Kiwi Salad Shots

Ingredients

1 kiwi fruit, peeled

1 apple, cored

1/2 cos lettuce

Juice of 1/2 lemon

SERVES 1

91 calories per serving

Method

Place all of the ingredients into a food processor with just enough water to cover them. Blitz until smooth. Pour the liquid into a glass bottle and keep it in the fridge, ready for you to have fresh shots throughout the day and a healthy drink between meals. Alternatively you can just drink it all straight away.

Pear Salad Smoothie

SERVES 1

83
calories
per serving

Ingredients

1 stalk of celery, roughly chopped

½ romaine lettuce, roughly chopped

1 large pear, cored

Method

Place all of the ingredients into a blender with sufficient water to cover them and blitz until smooth.

Superfood Juice

Ingredients

2 celery stalks

1 kale leaf

1 cucumber

1 apple

1 teaspoon chopped parsley

2.5cm (1 inch) chunk of ginger, peeled

1 lemon

1/4 teaspoon cinnamon (optional)

**SERVES
1**

128
calories
per serving

Method

Juice all the ingredients together and pour the juice into a tall glass. Stir in the cinnamon and drink immediately. You can add a few ice cubes for a really refreshing drink.

Green Goodness Smoothie

SERVES 1

242
calories
per serving

Ingredients

50g (2oz) spinach

1 pear, core removed

1/2 teaspoon of spirulina powder (optional)

1/4 cucumber

Flesh of 1/2 avocado

Method

Place the ingredients into a blender and pour in just enough cold water to cover them. Blitz until smooth and creamy. Serve and drink immediately.

Avocado & Banana Smoothie

SERVES 1

233
calories
per serving

Ingredients

Flesh of ½ avocado

1 small banana, peeled and roughly chopped

1 teaspoon peanut butter

Squeeze of lemon juice

Several ice cubes or crushed ice (optional)

Method

Place all of the ingredients into a blender and blitz until smooth. If your blender doesn't tolerate ice you can just add a few cubes.

Raspberry & Cashew Nut Crunch

Ingredients

100g (3½ oz) plain Greek yogurt

50g (2oz) raspberries

25g (1oz) unsalted cashew nuts, chopped

¼ teaspoon ground ginger

SERVES
1

291
calories
per serving

Method

Mash together half of the raspberries and all of the ginger with the yogurt. Using a glass, place a layer of yogurt with half of the remaining raspberries and a sprinkling of chopped cashews, followed by another layer of the same until you reach the top of the glass.

Ham & Tomato Mug Muffin

SERVES 1

203
calories
per serving

Ingredients

2 medium eggs

2 cherry tomatoes, chopped

1 slice of ham

1 teaspoon olive oil

1/4 teaspoon paprika

A few basil leaves, chopped

Method

Crack the eggs into a large mug and beat them. Add in the olive oil, ham, tomato, basil and paprika and mix well. Place the mug in a microwave and cook on full power for 30 seconds. Stir and return it to the microwave for another 30 seconds, stir and cook for another 30-60 seconds or until the egg is set. Serve it in the mug. Experiment with other ingredients, like chicken, prawns, bacon, beef, cheese, spring onions (scallions) and herbs.

17

Mushroom & Herb Omelette

Ingredients

75g (3oz) mushrooms, chopped

2 medium eggs, beaten

1 small handful spinach leaves, chopped

1 tomato, cut into slices

1 teaspoon fresh thyme leaves, chopped

1 teaspoon olive oil

SERVES 1

196
calories
per serving

Method

Heat the olive oil in a saucepan, add the mushrooms and cook until softened. Remove them and set aside. Pour the beaten eggs into the frying pan and allow them to set. Transfer the omelette to a plate and fill it with the mushrooms, spinach, tomato and herbs then fold it over. Enjoy.

Raspberry & Lemon Swirl

SERVES 1

208
calories
per serving

Ingredients

100g (3½ oz) plain Greek yogurt

50g (2oz) fresh raspberries

1 tablespoon ground flaxseeds (linseeds)

1 teaspoon lemon juice

Method

Place the raspberries into blender or food processor and blitz to a smooth purée. Place the yogurt into a bowl and mix in the flaxseeds (linseeds) and lemon juice. Add the raspberry purée and partly stir it in leaving swirls in the yogurt. Serve and enjoy.

Poached Eggs & Spinach

Ingredients

25g (1oz) fresh spinach leaves

2 medium eggs

1 teaspoon olive oil

Sea salt

Freshly ground black pepper

SERVES 1

178 calories per serving

Method

Scatter the spinach leaves onto a plate and drizzle the olive oil over them. Bring a shallow pan of water to the boil, add in the eggs and cook until the whites become firm. Serve the eggs on top of the spinach and season with salt and pepper.

Herby Mediterranean Scramble

Ingredients

- 2 medium eggs
- 1 tablespoon grated Parmesan cheese
- 1 tablespoon crème fraîche
- 1 teaspoon fresh basil leaves, chopped
- 1 teaspoon fresh oregano, chopped
- 1 teaspoon butter

SERVES 1

204 calories per serving

Method

Crack the eggs into a bowl, whisk them up. Add in the Parmesan cheese, crème fraîche, basil and oregano. Heat the butter in a frying pan. Pour in the egg mixture and stir constantly until the eggs are scrambled and set. Serve and enjoy.

Coconut & Lemon Yogurt

Ingredients

125g (4oz) plain Greek yogurt

1 tablespoon desiccated (shredded) coconut

1 teaspoon lemon juice

SERVES 1

258 calories per serving

Method

Place the yogurt in a serving bowl and stir in the coconut and lemon juice and stir well. Serve into a bowl and eat straight away.

Chocolate & Macadamia Yogurt

Ingredients

100g (3½oz) plain Greek yogurt

1 teaspoon 100% cocoa powder

6 macadamia nuts, chopped

SERVES 1

227 calories per serving

Method

Place the yogurt and cocoa powder into a bowl and stir until completely combined. Sprinkle the chopped nuts over the top. Serve and enjoy!

LUNCH
RECIPES

Prawn & Basil Savoury Muffin

Ingredients

25g (1oz) cooked peeled prawns (shrimps)

2 medium eggs

1 teaspoon olive oil

1 teaspoon fresh basil leaves, chopped

SERVES 1

216
calories
per serving

Method

Crack the eggs into a large mug and beat them. Add in the oil, prawns (shrimps) and basil. Place the mug in a microwave and cook on full power for 30 seconds. Stir and return it to the microwave for another 30 seconds, stir and cook for another 30-60 seconds or until the egg is set. Serve it in the mug.

Cheese & Olive Frittata

SERVES 2

249
calories
per serving

Ingredients

25g (1oz) pitted black olives, halved

25g (1oz) cheese, grated (shredded)

4 medium eggs, beaten

4 cherry tomatoes, halved

1 tablespoon fresh parsley, chopped

1 tablespoon fresh basil, chopped

2 teaspoons olive oil

Method

Whisk the eggs in a bowl and add in the parsley, basil, olives and tomatoes. Stir in the cheese. Heat the oil in a small frying pan and pour in the egg mixture. Cook until the egg mixture completely sets. You can finish it off under a hot grill (broiler) if you wish. Gently remove it from the pan and cut it into two. You can easily double the quantity of ingredients and store the extra portions to be eaten cold.

Chorizo Scramble

Ingredients

25g (1oz) chorizo sausage, chopped

25g (1oz) cheese, grated (shredded)

2 medium eggs, beaten

1 teaspoon olive oil

**SERVES
1**

379
calories
per serving

Method

Heat the oil in a frying pan and add in the chorizo. Cook for around 2 minutes. Pour in the beaten egg and stir, scrambling the eggs until completely cooked. Serve onto a plate and sprinkle with grated (shredded) cheese.

Paprika Prawn Tapas

Ingredients

300g (11oz) cooked peeled prawns

150g (5oz) chorizo sausage, chopped

3 garlic cloves, chopped

2 red chillies, deseeded, chopped

1 tablespoon smoked paprika

1 onion, finely chopped

2 tablespoons olive oil

SERVES 4

280 calories per serving

Method

Heat the oil over a frying pan and add in the onion, garlic, chillies and paprika. Cook for 5 minutes until the onions have softened. Add in chorizo and the prawns and cook for 5 minutes. If you are using frozen prawns make sure they are hot right through. Serve by itself or with a leafy green salad.

Parmesan Asparagus

Ingredients

200g (7oz) asparagus spears, trimmed

50g (2oz) Parmesan cheese, grated

1 tablespoon olive oil

Freshly ground black pepper

SERVES 2

191
calories
per serving

Method

Heat the olive oil in a frying pan or griddle pan, add the asparagus and cook for around 4 minutes, turning occasionally. Sprinkle the parmesan cheese on top of the asparagus and cook for another couple of minutes or until the cheese has softened. Serve and season with black pepper. Eat straight away, either on its own, or with a leafy green salad.

Asparagus & Poached Egg

Ingredients

- 150g (5oz) asparagus, tough end removed
- 50g (2oz) green salad leaves
- 1 large egg
- 1 tablespoon olive oil
- 1 tablespoon lemon juice
- Sea salt
- Freshly ground black pepper
- 1 teaspoon parmesan cheese, grated (shredded)
- Dash of vinegar

SERVES 1

245 calories per serving

Method

Lay the asparagus under a pre-heated grill and cook for 5 minutes on each side. Half fill a large saucepan with water and bring it to simmer. Add in the vinegar and stir. Crack the egg into a small side plate and slide it into the water. Cook for around 3 minutes until it firms up but remains soft in the middle. Combine the olive oil and lemon juice in a bowl and season it with salt and pepper. Coat the salad leaves with the dressing. Scatter the salad leaves on a plate, serve the asparagus on top and add the egg. Sprinkle with Parmesan cheese and eat straight away.

Mediterranean Tomato & Lentil Soup

Ingredients

400g (14oz) tin of chopped tomatoes
350g (12oz) tinned cooked lentils (drained)
1 onion, peeled and chopped
1 teaspoon tomato purée (paste)
1 teaspoon dried mixed herbs
1 tablespoon olive oil
900mls (1½ pints) hot vegetable stock (broth)
A large handful of fresh basil leaves, chopped
Sea salt
Freshly ground black pepper

SERVES
4

156
calories
per serving

Method

Heat the oil in a pan, add the onion and cook for 4 minutes. Add in the vegetable stock (broth), tomatoes, lentils and dried mixed herbs and bring it to the boil. Simmer for around 5 minutes. Stir in the basil. Use a food processor or hand blender and process until smooth. Season with salt and pepper. Serve and enjoy.

Red Pepper & Basil Soup

Ingredients

4 red peppers (Bell peppers), deseeded and chopped

3 cloves of garlic, crushed

1 onion, peeled and chopped

1 large tomato, chopped

1 carrot, peeled and finely chopped

1 large handful of fresh basil, chopped

600mls (1 pint) vegetable stock (broth)

600mls (1 pint) hot water

1 tablespoon olive oil

Sea salt

Freshly ground black pepper

SERVES 4

98 calories per serving

Method

Heat the oil in a saucepan. Add the onion, carrot and garlic and cook for 3 minutes. Add in the tomato and red peppers (bell peppers), hot water and stock and cook for 10 minutes. Add in the basil. Using a hand blender or food processor, blitz the soup until smooth. Season with salt and pepper. Serve and enjoy.

Beef & Mushroom Soup

SERVES 2

133 calories per serving

Ingredients

100g (3½ oz) cooked sliced beef, chopped

6 spring onions (scallions), finely chopped

4 large mushrooms, finely sliced

2 sticks of celery, finely chopped

2 teaspoons olive oil

600mls (1 pint) beef stock (broth)

Sea salt

Freshly ground black pepper

Method

Heat the oil in a saucepan, add the mushrooms, spring onions (scallions) and celery and cook for 3-4 minutes. Pour in the stock (broth) and chopped beef. Bring it to the boil, reduce the heat and cook for 10 minutes. Season with salt and pepper. Serve and enjoy.

Fast Tomato Soup

Ingredients

400g (14oz) tinned chopped tomatoes

2 spring onions (scallions), chopped

300mls (½ pint) vegetable stock (broth)

1 teaspoon balsamic vinegar

1 teaspoon olive oil

Sea salt

Freshly ground black pepper

**SERVES
1**

138
calories
per serving

Method

Heat the oil in a saucepan, add the spring onions (scallion) and cook for 2 minutes. Add in the tomatoes and stock (broth) and bring it to the boil. Add in a teaspoon of balsamic vinegar. Reduce the heat and simmer for 5 minutes until heated through. Using a food processor and or hand blender blitz until smooth. Season with salt and pepper. Enjoy.

Green Vegetable Soup

Ingredients

450g (1lb) broccoli, finely chopped

1 large leek, finely chopped

1 fennel bulb, finely chopped

1 courgette (zucchini), finely chopped

1 handful parsley, chopped

1 handful chives, chopped

Sea salt

Freshly ground black pepper

SERVES 4

61 calories per serving

Method

Place the broccoli, leek, courgette (zucchini) and fennel in enough boiling water to cover them and bring to the boil. Simmer for 8-10 minutes, until the vegetables are tender. Stir in the herbs. Using a hand blender or food processor blend until the soup becomes smooth. Add more water if required to adjust the consistency. Season with salt and pepper and serve.

Red Pepper & Chickpea Soup

Ingredients

200g (7oz) tinned chickpeas (garbanzo beans), drained

3 red peppers (bell pepper), de-seeded and chopped

2 teaspoons ground coriander (cilantro)

1 onion, peeled and chopped

1 handful of fresh parsley, chopped

1200mls (2 pints) vegetable stock (broth)

1 tablespoon olive oil

Sea salt

Freshly ground black pepper

SERVES 4

150 calories per serving

Method

Heat the oil in a large saucepan, add the onion and cook for 2 minutes. Add in the red peppers (bell pepper), ground coriander (cilantro) and stock (broth). Bring it to the boil, reduce the heat and simmer until the vegetables have softened. Using a hand blender or food processor and blitz until smooth. Return it to the saucepan, add the parsley and chickpeas (garbanzo beans) and warm them. Season with salt and pepper and serve.

Gazpacho

Ingredients

SERVES 4

122
calories
per serving

10 tomatoes, de-seeded and chopped

5 cloves of garlic, chopped

2 red peppers (bell peppers), de-seeded and chopped

2 medium cucumbers, peeled and chopped

1 teaspoon chilli flakes

4 tablespoons apple cider vinegar

2 teaspoons olive oil

Sea salt

Freshly ground black pepper

Method

Place all of the ingredients into a food processor or blender and blitz until smooth. If the soup is too thick, just add a little extra oil or vinegar. Eat straight away or chill in the fridge before serving.

Egg Drop Soup

Ingredients

SERVES 1

124 calories per serving

250mls (8fl oz) chicken stock (broth)

1 teaspoon olive oil

1 egg

1/4 teaspoon chopped garlic

Pinch of chilli flakes

Sea salt

Method

Heat the oil and chicken stock (broth) in a saucepan and bring it to the boil. Add in the garlic, chilli and salt and stir. Remove it from the heat. In a bowl, whisk the egg then pour it into the saucepan. Stir for around 2 minutes until the egg is cooked. Serve and eat immediately.

Asparagus Soup

SERVES 4

64
calories
per serving

Ingredients

375g (13oz) asparagus spears, tough end removed

2 cloves of garlic, chopped

1 handful of spinach leaves

1 teaspoon butter

750mls (1½ pints) warm vegetable stock (broth)

Method

Heat the butter in a saucepan, add the asparagus and garlic and cook for 4 minutes. Add in the spinach and vegetable stock (broth) and cook for 5 minutes. Using a hand blender or food processor blend the soup until smooth. Serve into bowls.

Creamy Chicken & Vegetable Soup

Ingredients

SERVES 4

188 calories per serving

275g (10z) cooked chicken (leftover roast chicken is ideal)

3 tablespoons crème fraîche

2 carrots, chopped (or you can use leftovers if you have them)

1 onion, finely chopped

1 tablespoon olive oil

1/2 teaspoon dried mixed herbs

1 litre (1 1/2 pints) vegetable stock (broth)

Method

Heat the oil in a saucepan, add the onion, carrots and mixed herbs and cook for 4 minutes. Add in the stock (broth) and chicken and bring it to the boil. Reduce the heat and simmer for 4 minutes. Stir in the crème fraîche. Using a hand blender or food processor blitz HALF of the soup until smooth, then return it to the saucepan, making sure it is warmed through before serving.

41

Avocado, Lime & Coriander (Cilantro) Soup

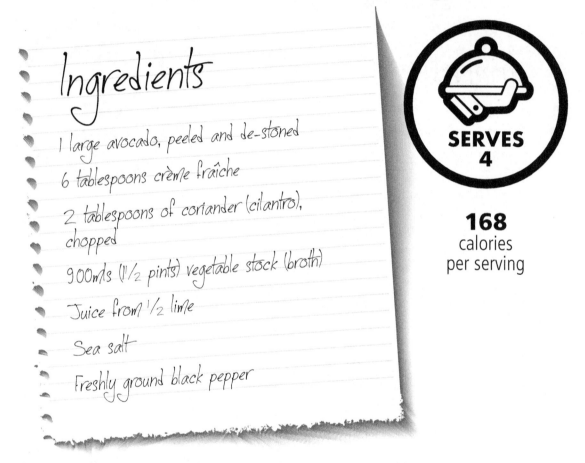

Ingredients

1 large avocado, peeled and de-stoned

6 tablespoons crème fraîche

2 tablespoons of coriander (cilantro), chopped

900mls (1½ pints) vegetable stock (broth)

Juice from ½ lime

Sea salt

Freshly ground black pepper

SERVES 4

168 calories per serving

Method

Place the avocado and half the crème fraîche into a blender and blitz until smooth. In a saucepan, heat the vegetable stock (broth) and add the remaining crème fraîche. Squeeze the lime juice into the avocado mixture and stir well. Gradually stir the avocado mixture into the warm vegetable stock, keeping it on a low heat until it is completely combined. Add in the coriander (cilantro) and season with salt and pepper. Serve into bowls. Eat straight away.

Turkey Soup

Ingredients

300g (11oz) cooked turkey (leftovers are ideal), cut into strips

200g (6oz) tinned chickpeas (garbanzo beans), drained

1 onion, peeled and chopped

1 red pepper (bell pepper), de-seeded and chopped

2 teaspoons ground coriander (cilantro)

2 teaspoons olive oil

1 handful of fresh basil, chopped

1½ litres (2¼ pints) vegetable stock (broth)

SERVES 4

242 calories per serving

Method

Heat the oil in a large saucepan, add the onion and cook for 2 minutes. Add in the red pepper (bell pepper), ground coriander (cilantro) and stock (broth). Bring it to the boil, reduce the heat and simmer for around 6 minutes. Stir in the turkey, chickpeas (garbanzo beans) and basil and warm it through. Serve into bowls and enjoy.

Red Pepper & Cannellini Soup

Ingredients

- 200g (6oz) tinned cannellini beans, drained
- 3 red peppers (bell pepper), de-seeded and chopped
- 2 teaspoons ground coriander (cilantro)
- 1 onion, peeled and chopped
- 1 small handful of fresh oregano, chopped
- 1 small handful of fresh parsley, chopped
- 1½ litres (2¼ pints) vegetable stock (broth)
- 1 tablespoon olive oil

SERVES 4

140 calories per serving

Method

Heat the oil in a large saucepan, add the onion and cook for 2 minutes. Add in the red peppers (bell pepper), ground coriander (cilantro) and stock (broth). Bring it to the boil, reduce the heat and simmer until the vegetables have softened. Using a hand blender or food processor and blitz until smooth. Return it to the saucepan, add the cannellini beans, oregano and parsley and warm it. Serve and enjoy.

Cannellini
& Courgette Soup

Ingredients

400g (14oz) tinned cannellini beans in water, drained

2 courgette (zucchini), de-seeded and finely diced

1 clove of garlic, chopped

1 onion, finely chopped

½ leek, halved, finely sliced and soaked in water

900mls (1½ pints) hot vegetable stock (broth)

100mls (3fl oz) milk

2 tablespoons olive oil

A large handful of fresh parsley, chopped

SERVES 4

207 calories per serving

Method

Heat the olive oil in a large saucepan. Add the onions, leek, courgette (zucchini), cannellini beans and cook for another 2 minutes. Pour in the hot stock and milk and cook for 10 minutes. Season with salt and pepper. Stir in the parsley and serve into bowls. Enjoy.

Creamy Tomato & Pesto Soup

SERVES 4

70 calories per serving

Ingredients

2 x 400g (14oz) tins of chopped tomatoes

2 cloves of garlic, peeled and chopped

2 teaspoons pesto sauce

1 teaspoon olive oil

360mls (12oz) vegetable stock (broth)

50mls (2oz) sour cream

Method

Heat the oil in a large saucepan. Add the garlic and cook for 1 minute. Pour in the tinned tomatoes and vegetable stock (broth). Bring it to the boil then reduce the heat and simmer for 5 minutes. Using a hand blender or food processor whizz the soup until it becomes smooth. Serve the soup into bowls. Add in 2 teaspoons of pesto and a dollop of cream and swirl it with a spoon before serving.

Quick Chicken & Mushroom Soup

Ingredients

200g (7oz) cooked chicken, chopped

4 medium mushrooms, finely chopped

4 spring onions (scallions) finely chopped

2 stalks of celery, chopped

1 tablespoon olive oil

1 tablespoon crème fraîche

600mls (1 pint) hot chicken stock (broth)

Sea salt

Freshly ground black pepper

SERVES 2

241
calories
per serving

Method

Heat the oil in a saucepan, add the mushrooms, celery and spring onions (scallions) and cook for 1 minute. Pour in the chicken stock (broth) and chopped chicken. Bring it to a simmer and cook for 8-10 minutes. Stir in the crème fraîche and season the soup with salt and black pepper. Serve and eat straight away.

Cucumber, Lettuce & Pea Soup

Ingredients

225g (8oz) frozen peas

8 spring onions, chopped

4 slices rye bread

1 cucumber, roughly chopped

1 lettuce, chopped

1800mls (3 pints) vegetable stock (broth)

1 teaspoon olive oil

SERVES 4

211 calories per serving

Method

Heat the oil in a large saucepan and add the spring onions. Cook for around 3 minutes, stirring occasionally. Add the peas, cucumber, lettuce and vegetable stock (broth) and simmer for 10 minutes. Using a hand blender or food processor, blitz the soup until smooth. Serve with a slice of rye bread. This soup can also be served cold.

Chilli Tomato King Prawns

SERVES 4

121 calories per serving

Ingredients

100g (3½ oz) pak choi (bok choy)

24 raw king prawns (jumbo shrimp), shelled

4 tomatoes, chopped

2 bird's eye chillies, chopped

2 tablespoons olive oil

1 tablespoon fresh coriander (cilantro), chopped

1 tablespoon fresh parsley, chopped

Method

Heat a tablespoon of oil in a frying pan and add in the prawns (shrimps) and cook until they are completely pink. Remove and set aside. Heat another tablespoon of oil in a pan and add the pak choi (bok choy), tomatoes and chilli peppers. Cook for 3 minutes. Return the prawns to the pan and warm through. Sprinkle with chopped coriander (cilantro) and stir. Serve with brown rice and salad.

Serrano & Rocket Salad

Ingredients

150g (5oz) Serrano ham

1 large handful of spinach leaves

1 large handful of rocket (arugula leaves)

1 tablespoons olive oil

1 tablespoon apple cider vinegar

1 tablespoon fresh orange juice

SERVES 2

224 calories per serving

Method

Pour the oil, vinegar and juice into a bowl and toss the spinach and rocket (arugula) leaves in the mixture. Serve the leaves onto plates and place the ham on top.

Lemon
& Pine Nut Asparagus

**SERVES
2**

149
calories
per serving

Ingredients

250g (9oz) asparagus spears, trimmed

1 tablespoon pine nuts

1 tablespoons olive oil

Juice of ½ lemon

Method

Coat a griddle pan or frying pan with olive oil. Lay out the asparagus spears on it and squeeze the lemon juice on top. Cook for 6 minutes, turning occasionally. Scatter the pine nuts into the pan and warm them slightly. Serve and eat straight away.

Smokey Bean & Quinoa Salad

Ingredients

300g (11oz) tinned cannellini beans, rinsed and drained

300g (11oz) cooked quinoa, cold

2 large handfuls of fresh coriander (cilantro)

1 handful of fresh chives, finely chopped

1 teaspoon smoked paprika

1 tablespoon olive oil

Juice of 1 lime

Sea salt

Freshly ground black pepper

SERVES 2

378 calories per serving

Method

Place the beans, quinoa, coriander (cilantro), chives (scallions), paprika, olive oil and lime juice into a bowl and mix well. Season with salt and pepper. Chill before serving.

Beetroot & Lentil Salad

Ingredients

- 200g (7oz) tinned cooked Puy lentils
- 100g (3½oz) cooked beetroot, chopped
- 2 tomatoes, deseeded and chopped
- 4 spring onions (scallions), finely chopped
- 1 small handful of parsley, chopped
- 1 small handful of fresh basil leaves, chopped
- 1 large handful of washed spinach leaves
- 2 cloves of garlic, finely chopped
- 1 tablespoon olive oil
- Juice and rind of 1 lime
- Sea salt
- Freshly ground black pepper

SERVES 1

389
calories
per serving

Method

Heat the olive oil in a saucepan, add the garlic and spring onions (scallions) and cook for 1 minute. Add the tomatoes, lentils, lime juice and rind. Cook for 2 minutes. Sprinkle in the herbs and stir. Scatter the spinach leaves onto plates. Serve the lentils onto the leaves. Scatter the beetroot on top. Season with salt and pepper.

Sweetcorn & Bean Salad

Ingredients

225g (8oz) tin of sweetcorn, drained

400g (14oz) tin of pinto beans, drained and rinsed

400g (14oz) tin of black-eyed beans, drained and rinsed

8 spring onions (scallions), chopped

4 tomatoes, chopped

1 handful of fresh coriander (cilantro) chopped

1 avocado, stone removed, peeled and diced

1 red pepper (bell pepper), chopped

1 green pepper (bell pepper), chopped

1 handful of fresh chives, chopped

1 clove of garlic, finely chopped

1 teaspoon sea salt

1 teaspoon paprika powder

1/2 teaspoon chilli powder (optional)

2 tablespoons olive oil

Juice of 1 lemon

SERVES 4

433 calories per serving

Method

Place the lemon juice, olive oil, paprika powder, garlic, salt and chilli in a bowl and mix well. In a large serving bowl, combine the beans, sweetcorn, avocado, tomatoes, peppers (bell peppers), spring onions (scallions), chives and coriander (cilantro). Pour the oil mixture over the salad ingredients and mix well before serving.

Grapefruit & Pine Nut Salad

Ingredients

1 tablespoons pine nuts

1 grapefruit, peeled, segmented and chopped

1 large handful of spinach leaves

1 large handful of rocket (arugula leaves)

1 tablespoon apple cider vinegar

1 tablespoons olive oil

1 tablespoon fresh orange juice

SERVES 2

145 calories per serving

Method

Pour the oil, vinegar and juice into a bowl and toss the grapefruit, spinach and rocket (arugula) leaves in the mixture. Serve with a sprinkling of pine nuts. Enjoy.

Feta & Watermelon Salad

Ingredients

150g (5oz) watermelon, skin removed & diced

50g (2oz) feta cheese, crumbled

1 shallot, finely chopped

Several mint leaves, finely chopped

Freshly ground black pepper

SERVES 1

176 calories per serving

Method

Place the watermelon, shallot, feta and mint leaves in a bowl and mix to combine all of the ingredients together. Season with a little black pepper and serve.

Tuna
& Cannellini Bean Salad

Ingredients

250g (9oz) cannellini beans, drained and rinsed

250g (9oz) tinned tuna

1 clove garlic, peeled and chopped

1 onion, peeled and finely chopped

1 tablespoon fresh basil, chopped

3 tablespoons lemon juice

1 tablespoon olive oil

**SERVES
2**

352
calories
per serving

Method

Place the lemon juice, olive oil and garlic into a bowl and stir well. Add the cannellini beans, tuna, onion and basil to the bowl and coat them in the oil mixture. Serve and eat straight away.

Greek Chicken Salad

Ingredients

- 75g (3oz) feta cheese, crumbled
- 50g (2oz) olives
- 2 tomatoes, chopped
- 2 cooked chicken breasts, chopped
- 1 small onion, chopped
- 1 romaine lettuce, chopped
- 1/2 cucumber, peeled and chopped
- 1 tablespoon fresh oregano, chopped
- 1 tablespoon fresh basil, chopped
- 1 clove of garlic, chopped
- 2 tablespoons apple cider vinegar
- 2 tablespoons olive oil
- Sea salt
- Freshly ground black pepper

SERVES 2

483 calories per serving

Method

Place the oil, vinegar, oregano, basil, garlic, salt and pepper into a bowl and mix well. Add the chicken, lettuce, cucumber, tomatoes, olives, onions and feta cheese and coat the ingredients in the oil mixture. Serve and enjoy.

Chilli Turkey & Avocado Salad

Ingredients

450g (1lb) turkey mince (ground turkey)

4 spring onions (scallions), chopped

2 Romaine lettuce, roughly chopped

2 tomatoes, chopped

1 red pepper (bell pepper), chopped

½ cucumber, chopped

2 avocados, skin & stone removed and chopped

1 teaspoon chilli powder

2 teaspoons paprika

1 teaspoon mixed herbs

2 cloves of garlic, peeled and chopped

1 tablespoon olive oil

Sea salt

Freshly ground pepper

SERVES 4

344 calories per serving

Method

Heat the olive oil in a frying pan, add the turkey and cook until it's no longer pink. Sprinkle in the paprika, chilli powder, mixed herbs, garlic and stir for 2 minutes or until the turkey is completely cooked. Scatter the lettuce, avocado, cucumber, tomato, pepper (bell pepper) and spring onions (scallions) onto plates. Spoon some of the turkey mixture on top of each salad. Season with salt and pepper. Serve and eat straight away.

Chickpea, Lemon & Coriander Salad

SERVES 2

140 calories per serving

Ingredients

400g (14oz) tin of chickpeas (garbanzo) beans, drained

4 tablespoon fresh coriander (cilantro)

2 spring onions (scallions) finely chopped

1 tablespoon lemon juice

Sea salt

Freshly ground black pepper

Method

Place the chickpeas (garbanzo beans) into a bowl and add in the coriander (cilantro), spring onions (scallions) and lemon juice. Mix the ingredients well. Season with salt and pepper. Eat straight away or store in the fridge until ready to use.

Feta Cheese & Butterbean Salad

Ingredients

400g (14oz) tin of butter beans

250g (9oz) cherry tomatoes, halved

125g (4oz) feta cheese, crumbled

75g (3oz) black olives, halved

2 tablespoons fresh basil, chopped

2 tablespoons fresh parsley, chopped

1 cucumber, diced

1 red onion, peeled and finely sliced

1 yellow pepper (bell pepper), diced

1 tablespoon olive oil

Juice of 1/2 lemon

SERVES 4

279 calories per serving

Method

Place the olive oil and lemon juice in a bowl and set aside. Place all of the salad ingredients into a large bowl and mix them together. Pour on the dressing and toss the salad ingredients in the mixture.

Quick Bean Chilli

Ingredients

- 400g (14oz) tin of mixed beans
- 400g (14oz) tin of chopped tomatoes
- 2 teaspoons ground cumin
- 1 teaspoon dried oregano
- ½ teaspoon smoked paprika
- ½ teaspoon chilli powder
- Sea salt
- Freshly ground black pepper

SERVES 2

250 calories per serving

Method

Place all of your ingredients into a saucepan, bring them to the boil and reduce the heat. Simmer for 10 minutes until the mixture is thoroughly warmed. Serve along with cauliflower rice and green salad.

Spanish Rice

SERVES 6

91 calories per serving

Ingredients

1 head of cauliflower, broken into florets.

2 carrots, peeled and roughly chopped

250g (9oz) tomato passata or tinned chopped tomatoes

2 tablespoons olive oil

1 teaspoon chilli powder

1 teaspoon cumin

Small handful of coriander (cilantro)

Method

Place the cauliflower and carrots into a food processor and blitz until fine and rice-like. Heat the olive oil in a large frying pan; add the cauliflower and carrots and cook for 5-7 minutes or until the vegetables have softened. Add the tomato passata and cumin and warm it through. Sprinkle in the coriander (cilantro) just before serving.

DINNER RECIPES

Chicken Fajitas, Salsa & Lettuce Wrap

Ingredients

FOR THE SALSA:
1 red onion, finely chopped

400g (14oz) tomatoes, chopped

2 garlic cloves, peeled and crushed

A large handful of fresh coriander leaves, chopped

Freshly ground black pepper

FOR THE CHICKEN FAJITAS
4 large chicken breasts, cut into strips

1 red onion, thinly sliced

1 red pepper (bell pepper) thinly sliced

1 yellow pepper (bell pepper) thinly sliced

1 large romaine lettuce, separated into leaves

1/4 teaspoon paprika

1/4 teaspoon mild chilli powder

1/4 teaspoon ground cumin

1/4 teaspoon dried oregano

1 tablespoon olive oil

SERVES 4

258 calories per serving

Method

FOR THE SALSA: Place all the ingredients for the salsa into a bowl and combine them. Season with pepper.
FOR THE FAJITAS: Heat the olive oil in a large frying pan, add the onion and peppers. Cook for 3 minutes until the vegetables begin to soften. Add in the chicken, paprika, cumin, chilli powder and oregano and stir well. Cook for around 6 minutes, or until the chicken is thoroughly cooked. Serve the chicken mixture inside a lettuce leaves and add a spoonful of salsa on top. Enjoy. You could also add guacamole or sour cream to your fajita.

Surf & Turf Steak With Prawns And Garlic Sauce

Ingredients

- 225g (7oz) peeled raw prawns (shrimps)
- 4 tablespoons crème fraîche
- 2 sirloin steaks (approx. 100g each)
- 2 tablespoons butter
- 1 tablespoon olive oil
- 3 cloves of garlic, chopped
- Sea salt
- Freshly ground black pepper

SERVES 2

400 calories per serving

Method

Sprinkle salt on each side of the steaks. Heat the oil in a frying pan, add the steaks and cook for 3-4 minutes, (or longer if you like them well done) turning once. Remove them from the pan and set them aside and keep them warm. Heat the butter to the pan, add the prawns (shrimps) and crème fraîche and cook for until the prawns are completely pink. Season with salt and pepper. Serve the steaks onto plates and spoon the prawns and sauce over the top. Eat straight away.

Chicken With Vegetable 'Spaghetti'

SERVES 2

268 calories per serving

Ingredients

- 2 cooked chicken breasts, roughly chopped
- 2 carrots
- 2 courgettes (zucchinis)
- 1 tablespoon olive oil
- 1 tablespoon fresh basil, oregano or parsley, chopped
- Sea salt
- Freshly ground black pepper

Method

Using a spiraliser to cut the carrots and courgettes (zucchinis) into strips. If you don't have a spiraliser, just use a vegetable peeler and cut into long then strips. Heat the oil in a frying pan, add the vegetables and cook for around 4 minutes. Add in the cooked chopped chicken and stir until it is warmed through. Season with salt and pepper. Sprinkle with fresh herbs and serve.

Tuna Steaks With Olives, Lemon & Basil Dressing

Ingredients

2 tuna steaks (approx. 100g each)

2 large handfuls of salad leaves

1 teaspoon olive oil

FOR THE DRESSING:

25g (1oz) pitted green olives, chopped

1 small handful of fresh basil leaves, chopped

1 tablespoon olive oil

Freshly squeezed juice of 1 lemon

SERVES 2

235 calories per serving

Method

Heat a teaspoon of olive oil in a griddle pan. Add the tuna steaks and cook on a high heat for 2-3 minutes on each side. Reduce the cooking time if you want them rare. Place the ingredients for the dressing into a bowl and combine them well. Scatter the salad leaves onto plates. Serve the tuna steaks with the dressing over the top.

Scallops & Pancetta

SERVES 1

240
calories
per serving

Ingredients

125g (4oz) large scallops, shelled

2 rashers of pancetta, chopped

1 teaspoon fresh parsley, finely chopped

1 clove of garlic, peeled and finely chopped

2 teaspoons olive oil

Sea salt

Freshly ground black pepper

Method

Heat 1 teaspoon oil in a frying pan over a high heat. Add the scallops and cook for around 1 minute on either side until they are slightly golden. Transfer to a dish and keep warm. Add the pancetta to the pan and cook for around 2 minutes. Add a teaspoon of olive oil and garlic and cook for around 1 minute. Sprinkle in the parsley. Serve the scallops onto a plate and spoon the pancetta and garlic butter on top. Season with salt and pepper.

Pork Béarnaise

Ingredients

250g (8oz) pork steaks

2 large handfuls of green salad leaves

2 teaspoons mustard

1 tablespoon fresh parsley, chopped

1 teaspoon butter

2 tablespoons double cream (heavy cream)

2 tablespoons red wine vinegar

Sea salt

Freshly ground black pepper

SERVES 2

318 calories per serving

Method

Season the pork with salt and pepper. Heat the butter in a frying pan and add the pork. Cook for around 3 minutes on either side. Remove the pork, set aside and keep it warm. Reduce the heat and add in the vinegar, mustard and cream and stir well. Sprinkle in the parsley. Serve the pork onto plates and pour the sauce over the top. Serve with green salad leaves.

Lemon Mustard Salmon & Lentils

Ingredients

250g (9oz) cooked Puy lentils

6 spring onions (scallions), chopped

2 salmon fillets

2 large tomatoes, chopped

1 small handful of basil leaves, chopped

2 large handfuls of rocket (arugula) leaves

2 teaspoons wholegrain mustard

1 teaspoon olive oil

Zest and juice of 1 lemon

SERVES 2

399 calories per serving

Method

Place the lemon juice and mustard in a bowl and stir. Coat the salmon steaks in the mustard mixture. Place them under a hot grill (broiler) and cook for around 6 minutes turning once in between until the fish is cooked completely. Heat a frying pan, add in the oil, lentils, spring onions (scallions) and tomatoes and cook for around 3 minutes or until warmed through. Stir in the basil leaves at the end of cooking. Serve the rocket (arugula) leaves onto plates and serve the lentils on top. Lay the cooked salmon on top of the lentils.

Pomegranate, Avocado & Chicken Salad

Ingredients

SERVES 2

423 calories per serving

- 2 cooked chicken breasts, chopped
- 2 avocados, peeled, de-stoned and chopped
- 3 spring onions (scallions) chopped
- 2 tablespoons fresh coriander (cilantro) leaves, chopped
- 2 large handfuls of green salad leaves
- 1 tablespoon lime juice
- Seeds of ½ pomegranate

Method

Place the avocado flesh and lime juice into a bowl and mix well. Add the spring onions (scallions), chicken and coriander (cilantro) and mix well. Scatter the salad leaves onto a plate and spoon the chicken and avocado mixture on top. Sprinkle with pomegranate seeds. Enjoy.

Turkey
Satay Skewers

SERVES 2

389 calories per serving

Ingredients

250g (9oz) turkey breast, cubed

25g (1oz) smooth peanut butter

1 clove of garlic, crushed

½ small bird's eye chilli, finely chopped

200mls (7fl oz) coconut milk

2 teaspoons soy sauce

Method

Combine the coconut milk, peanut butter, soy sauce, garlic and chilli. Add the turkey pieces to the bowl and stir them until they are completely coated. Push the turkey onto metal skewers. Place the satay skewers on a barbeque or under a hot grill (broiler) and cook for 4-5 minutes on each side, until they are completely cooked.

Hazelnut Crusted Salmon

Ingredients

25g (1oz) hazelnuts

2 teaspoons Dijon mustard

2 medium salmon fillets

1 large handful of fresh basil

1 teaspoon olive oil 1 tablespoon of olive oil

SERVES 2

387 calories per serving

Method

Place the nuts, mustard and basil into a food processor and mix until soft. Heat the olive oil in a frying pan, add the salmon fillets and cook for 4 minutes on one side. Turn the salmon over and spoon the mustard mixture on top of the salmon fillets. Cook for around 3 minutes, or until the fish feels firm. In the meantime heat the grill (broiler). Finish the salmon off by placing it under the grill to finish off for around 2 minutes. Delicious when served alongside roast vegetables or a leafy salad.

Creamy Parmesan Chicken

Ingredients

50g (2oz) Parmesan cheese, grated (shredded)

50g (2oz) spinach, chopped

4 chicken breasts, diced

2 cloves of garlic, peeled and chopped

200mls (7fl oz) crème fraîche

120mls (4fl oz) warm chicken stock (broth)

1 tablespoon olive oil

**SERVES
4**

362
calories
per serving

Method

Heat the oil in a frying pan, add the chicken and cook for around 5 minutes, stirring occasionally until it is cooked. Remove it and set aside, keeping it warm. Pour in the crème fraîche and add the garlic to the pan and stir. Add in the chicken stock (broth) and Parmesan cheese and stir until the mixture thickens. Scatter in the spinach and cook for around 2 minutes or until it wilts. Return the chicken to the pan to warm it through. This goes really well with vegetable 'spaghetti'.

Prawn, Avocado & Cannellini Salad

Ingredients

200g (7oz) cooked king prawns (shrimps)

150g (5oz) tinned cannellini beans

2 large handfuls of spinach leaves

1 avocado, peeled, de-stoned and chopped

1 teaspoon fresh coriander (cilantro) leaves, chopped

1/2 cucumber, chopped

1/2 teaspoon chilli powder

1/2 teaspoon paprika

Zest and juice of 1 lime

1 tablespoon olive oil

Freshly ground black pepper

SERVES 2

373 calories per serving

Method

Place the prawns into a bowl and sprinkle on the paprika and mix well. Place the chilli, lime juice and zest and oil in a bowl and stir well. Add in the cannellini beans, avocado, cucumber and coriander (cilantro) and toss them in the dressing. Serve the spinach onto plates and add the tossed salad with the prawns on top.

Tomato & Herb Chicken

Ingredients

400g (14oz) tinned chopped tomatoes

4 chicken breast fillets

2 cloves garlic, peeled and crushed

2 tablespoons tomato purée

1 onion, peeled and thinly sliced

1 small handful fresh basil leaves

1 teaspoon smoked paprika

1 teaspoon dried mixed herbs

1 tablespoon olive oil

1/4 teaspoon salt

1/4 teaspoon black pepper

SERVES 4

227 calories per serving

Method

Place the chicken in a bowl and sprinkle on the paprika, salt and pepper, coating it well. Heat the oil in a frying pan, add the chicken and brown it. Add in the garlic and onion and cook for 2 minutes. Add in the tomato purée (paste), tomatoes and herbs. Bring it to the boil then simmer gently. Stir in the torn basil leaves and make sure the chicken is completely cooked before serving.

Creamy Turkey & Leeks

SERVES 4

263
calories
per serving

Ingredients

450g (1lb) turkey steaks, chopped

250g (9oz) button mushrooms

250g (9oz) leeks, chopped

200mls (7fl oz) chicken stock (broth)

200mls (7fl oz) crème fraîche

4 tablespoons chopped fresh parsley

1 tablespoon olive oil

Method

Heat the olive oil in a large pan and add the turkey and mushrooms. Cook for 2 minutes, stirring constantly. Add in the leeks and stock (broth) and cook until the vegetables have softened and the turkey completely cooked. Add in the crème fraîche and warm it through. Sprinkle in the parsley before serving. This is delicious with cauliflower mash.

Creamy Avocado 'Courgetti'

Ingredients

- 1 tablespoon pine nuts
- 1 medium courgette
- 1 ripe avocado, peeled and stone removed
- 2 cloves of garlic, peeled
- 2 teaspoons olive oil
- 1 teaspoon lemon juice
- 1/2 teaspoon paprika
- Sea salt
- Freshly ground black pepper

SERVES 1

466 calories per serving

Method

Use a spiraliser or if you don't have one, use a vegetable peeler and cut the courgette (zucchini) into thin strips. Heat 2 teaspoons of oil in a frying pan, add the courgette (zucchini) and cook for 4-5 minutes or until it has softened. In the meantime, place the avocado, garlic, paprika, lemon juice and a teaspoon of olive oil into a blender and blitz the mixture until smooth. Add the avocado mixture to the pan with the courgette (zucchini) and stir it well until warmed through. Season with salt and pepper. Serve and sprinkle with pine nuts.

Smokey Bean Casserole

Ingredients

400g (14oz) haricot beans, drained and rinsed

400g (14oz) pinto beans, drained and rinsed

400g (14oz) tinned tomatoes, chopped

200g (7oz) button mushrooms, halved

3 garlic cloves, peeled and chopped

1 onion, peeled and chopped

1 tablespoon smoked paprika

1 teaspoon chilli powder

1 large handful of fresh coriander (cilantro)

250mls (8fl oz) hot vegetable stock (broth)

1 tablespoon olive oil

Freshly ground black pepper

SERVES 4

286 calories per serving

Method

Heat the oil in a saucepan, add the onions, mushrooms, garlic, chilli, beans, tomatoes and paprika and cook for 3 minutes. Pour in the stock (broth) and simmer for around 8 minutes or until the vegetables have softened. Stir in the fresh coriander (cilantro) and serve.

Prawn & Chorizo Stir-Fry

Ingredients

- 450g (1lb) king prawns (shrimp), peeled
- 75g (3oz) chorizo sausage
- 2 cloves of garlic, peeled and chopped
- 1 red pepper (bell pepper), chopped
- 1 green pepper (bell pepper), chopped
- 1 onion, peeled and chopped
- 1 courgette (zucchini), chopped
- ½ teaspoon chilli powder
- 50mls (2fl oz) chicken stock (broth)
- 1 teaspoon olive oil
- Sea salt
- Freshly ground black pepper

SERVES 4

208 calories per serving

Method

Heat the oil in a frying pan, add the prawns (shrimps) and cook for 3 minutes. Remove and set aside. Place the onion and peppers into a saucepan with the garlic and courgette (zucchini) and cook for 3 minutes. Add in the chorizo sausage and return the prawns to the pan. Cook for 2 minutes. Pour in the hot stock (broth) and add in the chilli. Season with salt and pepper. Make sure the ingredients are completely cooked. Serve and enjoy.

Chicken & Green Peppers

Ingredients

2 chicken breasts, chopped
2 handfuls of rocket (arugula) leaves
2 cloves of garlic, peeled and chopped
1 green peppers (bell peppers), chopped
1 onion, peeled and chopped
½ teaspoon paprika
½ teaspoon mild chilli powder
2 teaspoons olive oil
Sea salt
Freshly ground black pepper
2 teaspoons balsamic vinegar
Salt and freshly ground black pepper

SERVES 2

241
calories
per serving

Method

Place the chicken in a bowl and sprinkle on the paprika and chilli, making sure you coat it completely. Heat the oil in a large frying pan. Add the chicken and cook for around 3 minutes. Add in the onion, garlic, peppers and cook until the vegetables have softened. Scatter the rocket (arugula) on a plate and serve the chicken and vegetables on top. Season with salt and pepper. Eat straight away.

Garlic Prawns & Calamari

Ingredients

200g (7oz) king prawns (large shrimps), peeled

150g (5oz) calamari, cut into rings

3 cloves of garlic, peeled and chopped

1 red pepper (bell pepper), chopped

1 yellow pepper (bell pepper), chopped

1 large handful of rocket (arugula) leaves

½ teaspoon chilli flakes

1 tablespoon olive oil

A small bunch of coriander (cilantro), chopped

Method

Heat a tablespoon of olive oil in a frying pan or wok. Add the peppers and cook for 3-4 minutes or until they have softened. Remove them from the pan and keep them warm. Add the garlic, calamari, prawns and chilli to the pan and cook for around 2-3 minutes or until the prawns are pink throughout. Toss the peppers into the pan and coat them in the juices. Serve onto plates and place some rocket (arugula) leaves on the side. Enjoy straight away.

Lemon & Basil Chicken Skewers

SERVES 1

357 calories per serving

Ingredients

150g (5oz) chicken breast, cut into chunks

1 small bunch of basil, chopped

1 clove of garlic, peeled and chopped

Juice of ½ lemon

1 tablespoon olive oil

Sea salt

Freshly ground black pepper

Method

Place the oil, chopped basil, garlic and lemon juice in a bowl and mix well. Add the chicken to the marinade and stir well, covering the chicken completely in the mixture. Season with salt and pepper. Slide the chicken chunks onto metal skewers. Place them under a hot grill (broiler) or barbeque and cook for 5-6 minutes on each side or until the chicken is completely cooked through. Serve on its own or with salad and dips.

Smoked Salmon & Chicory Scoops

Ingredients

150g (5oz) red chicory leaves

150g (5oz) smoked salmon, finely chopped

100g (3½ oz) cucumber, diced

½ red onion, finely chopped

2 tablespoons fresh parsley, chopped

Juice of 1 lime

2 tablespoons olive oil

SERVES 4

145
calories
per serving

Method

Place the salmon, cucumber, onion, parsley, oil and lime juice into a bowl and toss the ingredients well. Separate out the chicory leaves then scoop the salmon mixture into them. Lay the chicory boats out on a plate and chill before serving.

Tomato & Mozzarella Skewers

SERVES 2

318
calories
per serving

Ingredients

12 cherry tomatoes, drained

1 handful of fresh basil leaves, chopped

12 mini mozzarella balls, drained

2 teaspoons olive oil

Salt and freshly ground black pepper

Method

Place the olive oil and chopped basil into a bowl and mix well. Add the mozzarella balls to the oil and coat them in the mixture. Thread the tomatoes and mozzarella alternately onto the skewers. Season with salt and pepper before serving.

Barbecued Mushrooms

SERVES 2

90
calories
per serving

Ingredients

3 cloves of garlic, peeled and chopped

2 large Portobello mushrooms, cleaned

1 tablespoons balsamic vinegar

1 tablespoons olive oil

Method

Remove the mushrooms stalks, chop them and place them in a bowl. Lay the mushrooms with the gills facing up. Place the garlic, balsamic vinegar and olive oil in a bowl and mix well. Spoon the mixture into the mushroom cap. Cook them on a barbecue for 8-10 minutes.

Mushroom Stroganoff

SERVES 4

165
calories
per serving

Ingredients

450g (1lb) closed cup mushrooms, washed and sliced

2 garlic cloves, peeled and crushed

1 onion, peeled and finely diced

1 teaspoon paprika

1/2 teaspoon mustard

250mls (9 fl oz) warm

vegetable stock (broth)

200mls (7fl oz) sour cream

1 tablespoon olive oil

Juice of 1/2 lemon

Sea salt

Freshly ground black pepper

Method

Heat the oil in a frying pan and add the onion. Cook for 5 minutes until the onion softens. Add the garlic and mushrooms and cook for 5 minutes until the mushrooms are golden. Stir in the paprika and mustard and cook for 1 minute. Pour in the stock (broth) and cook for 5 minutes. Pour in the sour cream and stir well, then add in the lemon juice. Season with salt and pepper. Serve with cauliflower rice.

DESSERTS, TREATS & SNACKS RECIPES

Blueberry, Coconut & Chia Seed Pudding

Ingredients

75g (3oz) blueberries

2 tablespoons chia seeds

1/2 teaspoon stevia

1/2 teaspoon vanilla extract

1/2 teaspoon ground cinnamon

100mls (3 1/2 fl oz) coconut milk

100mls (3 1/2 fl oz) almond milk

SERVES 4

79 calories per serving

Method

Place the coconut milk, stevia and vanilla extract into a bowl and mix until smooth. Add in the chia seeds and stir. Transfer the mixture to 4 dessert glasses or small bowls. Chill before serving. Sprinkle on the cinnamon and scatter the blueberries on top. Enjoy. These delicious little puddings can be stored in the fridge for 2-3 days.

Passion Fruit & Raspberry Mascarpone

Ingredients

50g (2oz) mascarpone cheese

50g (2oz) raspberries

Seeds of 1 passion fruit

A few extra raspberries to garnish

SERVES 1

235
calories
per serving

Method

In a large bowl, stir the seeds from the passion fruit into the mascarpone and mix well. Place the raspberries into a separate bowl and mash them to a pulp. Use a tall glass or dessert bowl and spoon in a layer of the mascarpone, then add a spoonful of the raspberry purée and swirl it slightly, repeat with another layer of mascarpone and raspberry until the mixture has been used up. Garnish with a few raspberries and serve.

Iced Banana
& Choc Chip Cream

Ingredients

3 frozen bananas, peeled

25g (1oz) smooth peanut butter

25g (1oz) cacao nibs

Pinch of sea salt

SERVES 2

276 calories per serving

Method

This is a super quick dessert which does require you to freeze some bananas in advance. Simply put the frozen bananas into a food processor and blitz until they become smooth. Add in the peanuts butter, cacao nibs and salt. Blend all of the ingredients.

Apple & Caramel Dip

SERVES 2

299 calories per serving

Ingredients

6 pitted dates

2 large apples, cored and sliced

1 teaspoon almond butter

120mls (4fl oz) hot water

Pinch of sea salt

Method

Place the dates, almond butter, water and salt into a food processor and combine them until the mixture is smooth and creamy. Spoon the mixture into a small serving bowl. Serve with the apple slices along with the dip.

Rhubarb & Ginger Compote With Greek Yogurt

Ingredients

200g (7oz) plain Greek yogurt

4 stalks of rhubarb, leaves removed and roughly chopped

2.5cm (1inch) chunk of fresh root ginger, peeled

Juice of 1 orange

1/2 teaspoon of stevia or to taste (optional)

SERVES 2

198 calories per serving

Method

Place the rhubarb chunks in a saucepan and add in the zest and juice of the orange together with the ginger and stevia (if using). Warm in gently until the rhubarb becomes soft and pulpy. Remove it from the heat and allow it to cool. Serve the yogurt into decorative bowls and serve the rhubarb compote on top.

Banana Frappuccino

SERVES 1

Ingredients

1 frozen banana

175mls (6fl oz) almond milk (or other milk)

1 teaspoon instant coffee

1 teaspoon 100% cocoa powder

1/2-1 teaspoon stevia power (optional)

143
calories
per serving

Method

Toss all of the ingredients into a blender and blitz until smooth. Drink it straight away and enjoy!

Coconut Balls

Ingredients

125g (4oz) almond butter

75g (3oz) macadamia nuts, chopped

75g (3oz) desiccated (shredded) coconut

1 tablespoon tahini paste (sesame seed paste)

1 teaspoon vanilla extract

1 teaspoon stevia sweetener (or more to taste)

Extra coconut for coating!)

MAKES 24

80 calories each

Method

Place the coconut, tahini (sesame seed paste), almond butter, vanilla extract and chopped macadamia nuts into a bowl and combine them thoroughly. Stir in a teaspoon of stevia powder then taste to check the sweetness. Add a little more sweetener if you wish. Roll the mixture into balls. Scatter some desiccated (shredded) coconut on a plate and coat the balls in it. Keep them refrigerated until ready to use.

Cherry
& Chocolate Milkshake

**SERVES
1**

233
calories
per serving

Ingredients

75g (3oz) frozen cherries, pitted

1 tablespoon 100% cocoa powder

Flesh of ½ avocado

100mls (3½ fl oz) almond milk (or other milk)

Method

Place all of the ingredients into a food processor or smoothie maker and process until smooth and creamy. Serve and enjoy.

You may also be interested in other titles by
Erin Rose Publishing
which are available in both paperback and ebook.

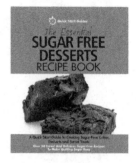

The Essential
HEALTHY GUT DIET
RECIPE BOOK

A Quick Start Guide To Improving Your Digestion, Health And Wellbeing
PLUS over 80 Delicious Diet-Friendly Recipes

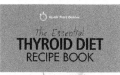

The Essential
Low FODMAP Diet
COOKBOOK

A Quick Start Guide To Relieving the Symptoms of IBS Through Diet
Improve Your Digestion, Health And Wellbeing
PLUS over 75 IBS Friendly Recipes!

The Essential
DIABETES DIET
COOKBOOK

A Quick Start Guide To Managing Your Diabetes Through Diet
PLUS over 100 Diabetic Friendly Recipes

ALKALINE DIET
SOLUTION

A Quick Start Guide To The Alkaline Diet
Lose Weight, Improve Your Health and Feel Great
PLUS over 90 Alkaline Friendly Recipes

The Essential
THYROID DIET
RECIPE BOOK

A Quick Start Guide To Healing Your Thyroid Through Diet, Lose Weight And Feel Great With Delicious Thyroid Friendly Recipes

The Essential
SIRT FOOD
DIET RECIPE BOOK

A Quick Start Guide to Cooking on the SIRT Food Diet!
Over 100 Easy and Delicious Recipes to Burn Fat, Lose Weight, Get Lean and Feel Great!

What Can I Eat?
ON A
DAIRY FREE
DIET

A Quick Start Guide To Quitting Dairy and Lactose
Lose Weight, Feel Great and Increase Your Energy
PLUS 100 Delicious Dairy-Free Recipes

LOWER CHOLESTEROL
DIET

A Quick Start Guide To Lower Cholesterol
Improve Your Health and Feel Great
PLUS over 100 Delicious Cholesterol Lowering Recipes

THE VEGAN 15 MINUTE
COOKBOOK

Over 100 Simple And Delicious Vegan Recipes For Everyone

The Essential
ROASTING TIN
COOKBOOK

Over 80 Easy And Delicious One Dish, No-Fuss Oven Recipes

Blood Sugar Diet
Diary

Daily Diary To Track Foods, Weight Loss And Wellbeing On the Blood Sugar Diet

Diabetes Diet
Diary

Daily Diary to Track and Record Diet, Blood Sugar and Well-being

My Diet Diary
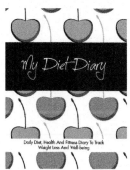

Daily Diet, Health And Fitness Diary To Track Weight Loss And Well-being

Low FODMAP
Food Diary
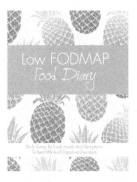

Daily Diary To Track Foods And Symptoms To Beat IBS And Digestive Disorders

Sugar-Free Diet
Diary

Daily Diary For Quitting Sugar, Losing Weight and Feeling Great

FOOD
Diary

Daily Diary To Track Diet And Symptoms To Beat Food Intolerances And Digestive Disorders

Printed in Great Britain
by Amazon